Mark Gerson

W. H. AUDEN

W. H. AUDEN

by

RICHARD HOGGART

Edited by Ian Scott-Kilvert

PUBLISHED FOR
THE BRITISH COUNCIL
BY LONGMAN GROUP LTD

LONGMAN GROUP LTD

Associated companies, branches and representatives throughout the world

First published 1957
Revised 1961, 1966, 1977

Revised editions © Richard Hoggart 1961, 1966, 1977

Filmset by Butler & Tanner Ltd
Frome and London
Printed in England by
Bradleys, Reading and London

ISBN 0 582 01093 4

CONTENTS

I. THE WANDERER 7

II. 1930 TO THE WAR YEARS: THE NEED FOR ORDER

(i) The Thirties in England 11
(ii) Politics, Psychology, 'Love' 14
(iii) Public and Private Speech 19

III. FROM THE FORTIES TO THE MID-FIFTIES: THE EXPLORATION OF FORMS

(i) 'Original Anxiety' 23
(ii) Symbolic Landscape and the Long Line 27

IV. FROM THE MID-FIFTIES TO 1973

(i) Divided Aims: The Game of Knowledge 35
(ii) Prose 39
(iii) Poetry and Companionability 42

¶ W. H. AUDEN was born in York on 21 February 1907 and died on 29 September 1973 in Vienna. He is buried in Kirchstetten, Lower Austria.

W. H. AUDEN

I. THE WANDERER

MANY of us who began our adult reading during the thirties in England will always think of W. H. Auden with a particular warmth, with the family sense we reserve for those writers who place their fingers on the pulse of a crucial period, whose writings are interwoven with our own intellectual and imaginative growing-up. We may differ in our judgements of his later work, but we agree in remaining grateful that at such a time he spoke about our common situation with intelligence and breadth, with urgency and energy and wit; that he spoke—to use a word he would probably have found congenial—'memorably'. Auden's middle-class and private jokes were as puzzling to some of us as they were to foreigners; but we responded to his high spirits and confidence, his novelist's interest in the details of social life, the exciting concreteness with which he captured salient features of the grey England of the raw suburbs and housing estates, the arterial roads and chromium-and-plastic cafés. With due scaling-down we can say of him what he said of Freud:

> To us he is no more a person
> Now but a whole climate of opinion.

We are not likely to forget the apt releasing force of such poems as 'Dover', 'Musée des Beaux Arts', 'Sir, No Man's Enemy' and 'A Shilling Life', or his vivid vigorous openings, or many scattered passages, such as:

> What do you think about England, this
> country of ours where nobody is well?

or,

> The vows, the tears, the slight emotional signals
> Are here eternal and unremarkable gestures
> Like ploughing or soldiers' songs:

or,

> May with its light behaving
> Stirs vessel, eye, and limb,

The singular and sad
Are willing to recover.

Yet, though Auden has held a high and special place in English poetic experience for more than four decades it is easy to feel some force in the argument that his illuminations are sometimes no more than heterogeneous surface-insights, and his technical skill more often showy than profound. Auden does occasionally employ certain fashionable clichés of tone and feeling: and he has been overrated in some literary circles. Just as surely, he has been underrated in others. Both attitudes tell something about contemporary cultural conditions in Britain. They tell less about the merits of Auden himself.

Auden remained intellectually and technically open and fluid (these are not polite euphemisms for 'fickle') to a degree that is not evident in any of those who were once known with him as 'the poets of the thirties'. His technical fluidity may be seen in his exercises in various poetic forms, especially after 1940. He practised, for instance, in *terza rima*, the *villanelle*, the sestina and the ballade. From this point of view the long poems *New Year Letter* (1941), *The Sea and the Mirror* (1945), *For the Time Being* (1945) and *The Age of Anxiety* (1948) are all aspects of the same formal search.

Yet this technical openness probably derives in part from a more radical quality, from an intellectual quixotry and eclecticism. Auden was something of an intellectual jackdaw, picking up bright pebbles of ideas so as to fit them into exciting conceptual patterns. He was evidently aware of this tendency and of one related to it; that is, of his inadequate submission to the 'this-ness', the immediate sensuous stuff, of life. More than once he refers with admiration to Rilke's 'acceptance', or insists that one must 'bless what there is for being', or that 'every poem is rooted in imaginative awe'. 'One must be passive to conceive the truth,' he says in 'Kairos and Logos'; and a fine metaphorical passage by Caliban in *The Sea and the Mirror* ('The shy humiliations ...') treats the same theme.

We can probably carry this same line of argument even further. For the intellectual unsteadiness seems to be a function of a yet deeper force: of a profound desire to come to ordered moral terms with life, and of a profound difficulty in doing so. *The Double Man* was the American title of *New Year Letter*. It is not one of Auden's best poems, though it has some moving lyric passages; it is nevertheless the fullest *exposition* of his philosophical problems. The American title was a peculiarly apt image for Auden's position at the time, and might still apply, though with less stress. Throughout his career, but with special force in the period before he became a professed Christian, Auden seems to have been an unusually divided man: searching for a belief towards which he could be truly humble, and finding humility difficult; questioning constantly the tensions within his own nature as both a fallen man and a creative artist. For Auden is primarily a purposive and moral writer. He is in the best sense a teacher, one who loves to influence others; on his weaker side he can be a somewhat gawky prose-moralizer. For him—the characteristic assertion indicates both a limitation and the source of much of his strength—'Art is not enough'.

Thus we may think of Auden in terms of one of his favourite images—that of the Wanderer, the man on a Quest. His poetry abounds in journeys over hills and across plains, in ascents of mountains and voyages across seas. The image appears in his very early adaptation of a Middle English poem, 'Sawles Warde':

> But ever that man goes
> Through place-keepers, through forest-trees,
> A stranger to strangers over undried sea

Variations occur throughout the thirties: in the Airman of *The Orators*, in poems such as 'Reader to Rider' and in the central characters of the plays *The Dog Beneath the Skin* and *The Ascent of F6*. Later, the same figure appears in the group of Quest sonnets printed in the one volume with *New Year Letter*, in *The Sea and the Mirror*, in *The Age of Anxiety* and in the libretto of *The Rake's Progress*. It is the theme of Auden's one full-length book of criticism, *The Enchafèd Flood*, in which the sea and the desert are considered as complex images of man's spiritual wanderings. Less sustained instances occur throughout all Auden's work, from the early 'mad driver pulling on his gloves' to 'A Change of Air' (in *About the House*).

In his final decade the Wanderer figure was not quite so prominent. Before then we might have been justified in saying, with many qualifications, that Auden was himself the Wanderer; the Wanderer pursuing the questions outlined above—of the 'double man' and, especially, of the double man as an artist.

Any one of a hundred passages could exemplify the first kind of question. The quotation below has been deliberately chosen at random from the *Collected Shorter Poems* so as to indicate the frequency of the theme:

In my own person I am forced to know
How much must be forgotten out of love,
How much must be forgiven, even love.

The second question is raised most strikingly in Auden's elegies on other writers; as in these lines on Henry James:

All will be judged. Master of nuance and scruple,
Pray for me and for all writers living or dead;
  Because there are many whose works
Are in better taste than their lives; because there is no end
To the vanity of our calling: make intercession
  For the treason of all clerks.

Because the darkness is never so distant,
And there is never much time for the arrogant
  Spirit to flutter its wings . . .

Yet it is important to notice that the Quest is not undertaken for its own sake. That would be a romantic delusion, and Auden never had much patience with the self-regarding romantic personality. The Quest is for order, for pattern and meaning, in life.

The constant interaction of all the qualities we have briefly outlined—Auden's great technical skill (in particular his fine ear and sense of timing); his remarkably acute eye for revealing detail; his intellectual responsiveness, liveliness and range; his search for spiritual order—all these combine to produce Auden's characteristic tones and themes:

The earth turns over; our side feels the cold;
And life sinks choking in the wells of trees:
The ticking heart comes to a standstill, killed;
The icing on the pond waits for the boys.
Among the holly and the gifts I move,
The carols on the piano, the glowing hearth,
All our traditional sympathy with birth,
Put by your challenge to the shifts of Love.

. . .
Language of moderation cannot hide:—
My sea is empty and its waves are rough;
Gone from the map the shore where childhood played,
Tight-fisted as a peasant, eating love;
Lost in my wake the archipelago,
Islands of self through which I sailed all day
Planting a pirate's flag, a generous boy;
And lost the way to action and to you.

Lost if I steer. Tempest and tide may blow
Sailor and ship past the illusive reef,
And I yet land to celebrate with you
The birth of natural order and true love:
. . .

II. 1930 TO THE WAR YEARS: THE NEED FOR ORDER

(i) *The Thirties in England*

Few recent decades in English life have, retrospectively, so boldly defined a character as the thirties. They seem now like a rising wave after a trough, a wave which preceded disasters.

In domestic affairs the keynote was struck in America, with the Wall Street crash of 1929. From the time this recession reached England until the rearmament boom of the decade's last years, unemployment was an ever-present feature of English life. This was the period of the 'Depressed Areas', of what Auden called 'the Threadbare Common Man/Begot on Hire-Purchase by Insurance', of 'smokeless chimneys, damaged bridges, rotting wharves and choked canals'. It was a period when shabby-genteel clerks could be found selling gimcrack Japanese household sundries from door-to-door. It was a grey and squalid period, especially for the millions directly affected by unemployment.

Internationally the starting-point lies in earlier events, but may be conveniently taken as Hitler's assumption of the German Chancellorship in 1933. Thereafter, as is clear now, there was a giant's march to the explosion of September 1939. The crucial midway stage was the opening of the Spanish Civil War in 1936.

For most young English people with left-wing interests this was a period of fervent left-wing (or of pacifist) activity, of Popular Front meetings, of milk for Spain and aid for Basque refugees, and of Mr Victor Gollancz's Left Book Club publications. It was marked by a more than usually strong feeling that 'the old gang' were appallingly unaware of the changing world situation. It was, in Auden's phrase, a 'time of crisis and dismay'.

Yet in the apparent simplicity of its issues and in the dramatic or even symbolic quality of its detail (unemployed men standing idle under the lamp-posts at street corners; the International Brigade; Guernica) it was a peculiarly heady period. It was in a certain sense enjoyable precisely because of its comparatively clear-cut moral situations and general all-hands-on-deck air. Such a period could call out the best qualities, as well as the more naïve enthusiasms, of concerned young Englishmen in all classes; and notably of that traditionally concerned group, the intelligent professional middle-class at the Universities.

To this class Wystan Hugh Auden belonged. Born in 1907 in York, Auden was the son of a medical officer with wide general and literary interests. His mother was a devout Anglo-Catholic. Subsequently the family moved to the great Midland city of Birmingham, and here no doubt Auden later gained much of his first-hand experience of economic depression. Here too he probably first discovered the unfailing fascination which 'the soiled productive cities' had for him, the pull of the great urban sprawls of the commercial Western world (Pittsburgh, Manchester, Detroit, the Ruhr). 'My heart has stamped on / The view from Birmingham to

Wolverhampton', he said in a light poem he later rejected, and, 'Tram-lines and slag-heaps, pieces of machinery / That was, and is, my ideal scenery'. 'Nothing is made in this town,' he said of Dover, and the implication was plainly pejorative.

At Gresham's School, Holt, Auden talked first of becoming an engineer and read technological works, chiefly on mining and geology. But in his early teens, prompted by a friend, he began to write poetry. Hardy was his first master—an admirably humane man and a magnificently varied and idiosyncratic versifier who yet is rarely so completely successful as to discourage a young practitioner. At Christ Church, Oxford, Auden had reached the stage at which he could one day tell his tutor, with an impressive confidence, that only Eliot was worth the serious consideration of poetic aspirants. But this was one necessary moment in a poet's development and there were other influences, notably Anglo-Saxon and Middle-English poetry which continued to fascinate Auden. At Oxford, too, Wilfred Owen and Edward Thomas were admitted to the accepted canon of ancestors for his generation. Auden's friendship with Stephen Spender began (and had about it, typically, something of the English public schools' prefect-to-fag relationship); and his first links were made with others who were to become writers and publicists in what has variously been called the Thirties Group, the Pylon School and the Auden Group. Incidentally, the group were united more by common assumptions and written influence than by actual meetings. The three best-known poets of the group, Auden, Spender and Day Lewis, did not meet as a trio until the late forties, at a cultural conference in Venice.

After a stay in pre-Hitler Berlin there followed for Auden a short period of school-teaching, which he seems to have deeply enjoyed. He had, we have already implied, a strong charismatic sense, a good teacher's love and firmness, energy and fidelity. Meanwhile, his first volume of poems had been published in 1930 and been followed by *The Orators*, an acute, fantastic and vigorous squib. In 1935 he married Erika Mann. As the decade progressed he became more and more engaged, not only in his craft as a poet but in the time-consuming borderland where political affairs and the practice of writing mingle. A largely light-hearted visit to Iceland with Louis

MacNeice in 1936 was followed by visits to Spain in 1937, to China and the U.S.A. with Christopher Isherwood in 1938. A few months before the beginning of World War II Auden settled in America, and in due time adopted American citizenship.

(ii) *Politics, Psychology, 'Love'*

Centring the eye on their essential human element

Some critics suggest that Auden is a peculiarly English poet, and that in leaving England he severed essential roots. The first suggestion is to a large extent true, in both more and less obvious senses. Local and family concerns are very dear to Auden; and his bedside book in New York was a work on the mineralogy of the Lake District. More, the cast of Auden's mind has markedly been formed by some of the main elements in the English tradition. His is not a voice from the Middle West or from Central Europe: 'England to me is my own tongue.'

Yet does the second suggestion—that Auden weakened his poetry by a physical removal—necessarily follow? Wherever he lived the bent of Auden's mind, the way he approached the problems which interested him—his particular form of complicated cranky independence as well as his tough gentleness—remained recognizably English. But the nature of these problems had something to do with the decision as to where he might best live. Auden's interest was in men in urban societies, in men living through their perennial moral and metaphysical problems in megalopolitan settings. London or some large English provincial city might have provided such a setting; but England is small and domestically intimate, its cultural life demandingly homely. Auden needed a kind of anonymity within an urban mass, and this New York provided (as well as providing sufficient money and the friendships Auden needed):

> More even than in Europe, here,
> The choice of patterns is made clear
> Which the machine imposes, what
> is possible and what is not,
> To what conditions we must bow
> In building the Just City now.

Auden is a socially unrooted poet who could have been at home in any of the large urban centres of the Western hemisphere. Whatever he might have lost by leaving England was not central to these gifts: in America, he seemed understandably to feel, he was at the chief pressure-point of forces which are changing the face of life in the West.

Auden's isolation in a crowd reflects a constant quality of his verse, a quality most plainly indicated in the early figures of the Hawk and the Airman (*The Orators*). The Airman was physically isolated from the messy close disorder of life below and, more important, able from his post of observation to detect therein some pattern not visible to those immersed in the details of personal involvement. Similarly, Auden's is often an abstracting and generalizing intelligence. In some sense very difficult to define fairly we may say that he is emotionally detached from much of what he describes, that he has a 'clinical' quality.

Though Auden speaks to and for many in his generation his speech commonly lacks certain kinds of intimacy. There are important areas of experience, particularly those concerned with relations between the sexes, which he either does not touch or touches in a perfunctory or stereotyped or briskly impersonal manner (falling in love, married life, some forms of insecurity, the tragic, gay and dignified tensions in the day-to-day life of 'ordinary' people). At such points he is likely to move into a detached 'placing' of detail by the use of successive definite articles:

> The boarding-house food, the boarding-house faces,
> The rain-spoilt picnics in the windswept places,
> The camera lost and the suspicion,
> The failure in the putting competition,
> The silly performance on the pier ...

A poet's weaknesses are often peculiarly revealing. There are forms of emotional wobble in, say, Tennyson, or of anger and enthusiasm in Browning, or of sensuous indulgence in Dylan Thomas, which at once limit them and bring them closer to us. In Auden's poetry, there are certainly struggles, but they are expressed through a continuous *argument* with the self rather than through the play of personal emotions. The 'I' is there, but is rarely at a loss with itself; it may be exploring its own weaknesses but always does so with an air of control, with the implication that certain areas are sealed-off and the limits of the struggle grasped. These are the roots Auden lacks and would have lacked even if he had remained in England.

This quality seems related to the fact that Auden's poems tend to be remembered not so much for their sensuous effects (apart from a few striking exceptions) as for the articulation of their phrasing and the pattern of their moral insights. His poems have little colour, smell or touch. He once said that he tends to think of them as 'squares and oblongs'; that is, as geometric shapes rather than as, for example, extended images. The bare shapes are the shapes of his dialectic. Similarly, his epithets usually have a conceptual rather than a sensuous relationship to the nouns they qualify; they comment rather than describe. Where several epithets are used they do not cumulatively describe their noun so much as set up an intellectual friction with the noun and with each other:

> And the active hands must freeze
> Lonely on the separate knees.

Auden does not say 'green slope' or 'grassy slope' but 'tolerant enchanted slope'; a lover's head on his arm is caught, beautifully, as a moral pattern rather than a visual:

> Lay your sleeping head, my love,
> Human on my faithless arm.

Again, though Auden's similes are rhetorical, and often boldly rhetorical, they usually gain their effect from the yoking of an abstract idea to a vividly concrete fact, from a vivid metaphorical personification of ideas:

> Problems like relatives standing

and,

> Will Ferdinand be as fond of a Miranda
> Familiar as a stocking?

And Auden's geography is almost always economic or political geography; thus his poem about the Chinese port of Macao opens—'A weed from Catholic Europe, it took root'. Or his landscapes are symbols of human dilemmas.

A varied intelligence, a congenitally pattern-making mind and a persistent moral drive: all these place the emphases in Auden's work firmly on man rather than nature, and on man-in-the-city rather than man-in-the-fields. It was inevitable that in the thirties Auden should pursue his psychological and social interests, should be purposively trying to create an order in his experience:

Our hunting fathers told the story
  Of the sadness of the creatures,
Pitied the limits and the lack
  Set in their finished features;
Saw in the lion's intolerant look,
Behind the quarry's dying glare,
Love raging for the personal glory
  That reason's gift would add,
. . .

Who, nurtured in that fine tradition,
  Predicted the result,
Guessed Love by nature suited to
  The intricate ways of guilt . . .?

The bent of Auden's political interests ensured that he was often thought, mistakenly, to be a Marxist. He did find much to admire in Marxist analysis; the argument that 'freedom is the recognition of necessity' alone would have won his interest. He did work, incidentally, for left-wing causes ('the expending of powers / On the flat ephemeral pamphlet and the boring meeting'). Of this kind of poem the most representative, whether by Auden or by any of the engaged poets of the thirties, was 'Spain 1937' with its characteristic refrains:

. . . Yesterday all the past

. . . Tomorrow, perhaps, the future . . .

. . . But today the struggle . . .

But for Auden this activity was inspired chiefly by his urgent search for spiritual order and moral responsibility. At bottom his attitude had more in common with that of some conservative and right-wing intellectuals than with that of the more progressive, 'free' and romantically expectant left-wing intellectuals of the thirties.

And his psychological interest was deeper than his political interest. Why were so many out of love with themselves? How had we become a nation of 'aspirins and weak tea'? At this stage Auden was predominantly interested in the plight of the specifically neurotic, of 'the lost, the lonely, the unhappy', of 'the malcontented who might have been', of the anxious and fear-ridden. The interest remains, but long ago widened into a concern with a more radical anxiety. In the thirties Auden's reading of Freud and Groddeck notably, encouraged a kind of modern myth-making, since both these writers communicate an unusual imaginative excitement in their presentation of concepts themselves richly suggestive:

> Sir, no man's enemy, forgiving all
> But will his negative inversion, be prodigal:
> Send to us power and light, a sovereign touch
> Curing the intolerable neural itch,
> The exhaustion of weaning, the liar's quinsy,
> And the distortions of ingrown virginity.
> Prohibit sharply the rehearsed response
> And gradually correct the coward's stance:

The address to a negatively defined power was an early indication that politics and psychology were only aspects of a more central interest, of Auden's concern with the spiritual dilemmas of individuals beyond the reach of political and psychological reforms. This is, of course, a religious interest; and though it showed itself plainly only towards the end of the decade it had many earlier intimations. Particularly, Auden returns again and again to a single word, 'Love'—and uses it elusively:

> O Love, the interest itself in thoughtless Heaven ...

and,

> The word is Love
> Surely one fearless kiss would cure
> The million fevers ...

and,

> Birth of a natural order and of Love ...

'Love' seems to have been an undefined but powerful third force, a quality both inside man and affecting man from outside, which at once offered him hope and indicated the perennial and personal nature of his situation. The history of Auden's earlier mental journey is, roughly speaking, that of the gradual discovery of the potentialities of this word's meaning for him—from an unresolved assertion to a rich and complex ambiguity which embraces the idea of Christian love, of conscience, of charity and grace. When that moment was reached Auden was an avowed Christian. The more directly political and psychological interests had fallen into place and the first phase was over. It is easy to exercise hindsight in such matters. In Auden's development the lines are clear and expressed:

> Perhaps I always knew what they were saying;
> Even the early messengers who walked
> Into my life from books ...
> Love was the word they never said aloud ...
> And all the landscape round them pointed to
> The calm with which they took complete desertion
> As proof that you existed.
> It was true.

(iii) *Public and Private Speech*

There is a small body of Auden's very early verse whose qualities are different from those we normally associate with his poetry in the thirties. These poems are dry and gnomic:

> Love by ambition
> Of definition
> Suffers partition
> And cannot go
> From yes to no
> For no is not love, no is no ...

Since the impulse behind these poems is close to that which informs some of Auden's poems of the fifties, we are reminded once more of the coherence of his intellectual development. But in the thirties Auden was more characteristically a poet of perceptive epigrammatic verse, of various kinds of conversational metre and of a number of remarkable lyrics.

The epigrammatic manner clearly took force from Auden's purposively ranging mind and from his insistent rhetorical inclinations. The epigrams usually enshrine memorable social and psychological observation, sometimes not so much crisp as slick, but generally intelligent and pithy:

> Steep roads, a tunnel through the downs are the
> approaches;
> A ruined pharos overlooks a constructed bay;
> The sea-front is almost elegant; all this show
> Has, somewhere inland, a vague and dirty root:
> Nothing is made in this town.
>
> But the dominant Norman castle floodlit at night
> And the trains that fume in the station built on the sea
> Testify to the interests of its regular life:
> Here live the experts on what the soldiers want
> And who the travellers are, ...

Poems such as this are among the more notable instances of the way in which the climate of the thirties could affect a well-equipped poetic mind. There were other manners of 'speaking to the times' which said more for the earnestness of the poet's intentions than for their grasp of poetry's function. We may grant that society was 'sick' and that the poets urgently wished to contribute usefully. Yet by the nature of contemporary culture they spoke only to a small minority. How could they speak more widely? Could they in any proper way compete with the truly popular voices?

To this aspect of Auden's work belong the three plays he wrote with Christopher Isherwood and Louis MacNeice between 1935 and 1938. In some of their techniques for presenting social problems and for obtaining a sense of urgent participation from the audience they seem to have learned something from the early 'epic theatre' of the German Communist playwright Bertolt Brecht. They made use also of hints from German expressionism, from popular songs and variety and music-hall performances. The plays were lively, intelligent and witty. To those, out of love with a glossy commercial theatre, who saw them at Rupert Doone's Group Theatre in London, they must have been unusually exciting. But they have the faults of their originating assumptions. They are lively charades with passages of striking banality and pert 'knowingness'. Their characters are not merely 'types'—

that may be true of certain good plays. But they are usually cliché-ridden or idea-ridden types, Freudian or Marxian puppets. All of them have some good lyrics and choruses, but only *The Ascent of F6* is now worth close attention. In this play the 'Quest' theme, because it is more deeply probed, inspires some scenes much more searching and eloquent than any in *The Dog Beneath the Skin*.

During the thirties Auden's demotic interests best served his poetry in the practice of the epigrammatic line and of various conversational metres. In the latter he aimed at a laconic and loose-limbed, a dryly ironic or apparently off-hand tone of voice. The tone had begun to appear by the middle thirties, as in the unbuttoned, *in medias res*, colloquially reflective opening of 'Musée des Beaux Arts':

About suffering they were never wrong,
The Old Masters: how well they understood
Its human position; how it takes place
While someone else is eating or opening a window
or just walking dully along; ...

...
In Brueghel's *Icarus*, for instance: how everything turns away
Quite leisurely from the disaster; the ploughman may
Have heard the splash, the forsaken cry,
But for him it was not an important failure; the sun shone
As it had to ...

For this manner (especially as it was adopted in his often admirable symbolic sonnets) Auden took much from Rilke. But the most important creditor was Yeats, whose conversational metres Auden most perceptively praised. Yeats's 'Easter 1916' begins:

I have met them at close of day
Coming with vivid faces
From counter or desk among grey
Eighteenth-century houses.

The echo can be plainly heard (though really in no more than a very competent imitation) in Auden's '1st September 1939':

I sit in one of the dives
On Fifty-Second Street

Uncertain and afraid
As the clever hopes expire ...

The conversational manner was predominant in *Another Time* (1940). Subsequently, it was influenced by Auden's experience in America, where the rhythms of colloquial speech often seem more flexible than they are in England:

The sailors come ashore
Out of their hollow ships,
Mild-looking middle class boys
Who read the comic strips:
One baseball game is more
To them than fifty Troys.

They look a bit lost, set down
In this unamerican place ...

Since this is essentially a relaxed manner it sometimes encouraged Auden's characteristic technical faults, and so became slipshod rather than relaxed, slick instead of laconic, informedly glib rather than finely allusive. At its best its shrewdly loose articulation allowed it to carry very effectively the intelligent, unviatic, contemporary observations Auden often wished to make.

Most of the foregoing comments on Auden's style have had a bearing on his social and psychological interests. His lyrics exist much more in their own right, and spring from simpler but very firm poetic roots. This is an aspect of Auden's work which his evident moral drive can easily lead us to underrate. Auden's admirable lyrics have been a continuous feature of his verse, from a fine group in the mid-thirties which included such poems as 'O who can ever praise enough' to 'Deftly, Admiral' (*Nones*). We remember here also the quick and witty choral songs such as 'At last the secret is out', the comic and satiric poems such as 'O for doors to be open', the Nonsense Rhyme in *Nones* and the recent 'Willow-Wren and the Stare'. The note which seems most characteristic and most impressive in the lyrics is of a kind of stillness; not a passivity nor always the stillness of menace, but a held imaginative stasis where the spirit looks steadily and often tenderly at a still moment of experience. It is all, of course, as much a matter of sound as of sense:

Dear, though the night is gone,
Its dream still haunts today . . .

and,

Fish in the unruffled lakes
The swarming colours wear . . .

and,

Deftly, admiral, cast your fly
Into the slow deep hover . . .

and,

Now the leaves are falling fast,
Nurse's flowers will not last;
Nurses to the graves are gone,
And the prams go rolling on.

Whispering neighbours, left and right,
Pluck us from the real delight;
And the active hands must freeze
Lonely on the separate knees.

III. FROM THE FORTIES TO THE MID-FIFTIES: THE EXPLORATION OF FORMS

(i) *'Original Anxiety'*

From 1940 to the mid-fifties, Auden moved around the American continent fairly consistently, chiefly as a lecturer and teacher at universities and colleges. Then, from 1956 to 1961, he was Professor of Poetry at Oxford and so spent some time regularly in England. From 1949 to 1957 he had a spring and summer home on Ischia, the island off Naples. That yielded in 1958 to his house in Kirchstetten, Lower Austria (again, for spring and summer). He died en route from there to Oxford where, at Christ Church, he had a 'grace and favour' cottage in the last year of his life. But for more than thirty years—from 1939 to 1972—Auden's home-base or point of rest was overwhelmingly New York.

The move to America roughly coincided with the clear and frequent appearance in Auden's poetry of a number of new influences. If Freud and Marx were the most striking and typical intellectual influences of the thirties, then those of the forties were Kierkegaard and Reinhold Niebuhr.

The exploration by the Danish 'existentialist' theologian Søren Kierkegaard of 'original anxiety', the basic insecurity of man which marks both his fallen condition and his possible salvation, this in particular replaced for Auden—as a fruitful area of thought and a seminal metaphor—the psychologists' more scientific analysis of the nature of anxiety. 'Psychotherapy will not get much further until it recognizes that the true significance of a neurosis is teleological,' Auden now said.

Similarly, Reinhold Niebuhr's analysis of the moral dilemmas and social involvements of man submerged Auden's rather scrappy and qualified interest in Marxism. Niebuhr was, from 1930–60, Professor of Applied Christianity at the Union Theological Seminary, New York; the most accessible exposition of his outlook is in the two volumes of Gifford Lectures, *The Nature and Destiny of Man*. Auden's sense of continuous struggle in the will makes it easy to understand why he should have been drawn to Niebuhr's form of Protestantism—Auden was in fact a Protestant Episcopalian. We may assume that he would have been in sympathy with this statement by Niebuhr: 'The Catholic emphasizes the initial act of intellectual assent; the Protestant the continuous process of voluntary assent.' Nor was Auden's awareness of society likely to allow him ever to become mystical or contemplative.

Such statements are bound to over-simplify; there are obviously many other interweaving lines of force. But these were the dominant and most revealing forces at this time. Auden quoted Kierkegaard repeatedly, in his poetry and prose; and some of his poems of the forties are like versified paragraphs of Niebuhr.

Auden's social and psychological interests remained, but were related now to a central religious root. Man is seen as fallen yet free, and this is his paradox. He is bound by his 'creatureliness' yet always tempted to deny the limitations this imposes; he is free to exercise moral choice for good or ill. Hence his 'wilfulness' in both the senses of 'possessing free will' and 'prompt to disobey'. He works out his destiny here, historically, in time; his consciousness of time informs his awareness of guilt and of possible grace. This awareness marks man's unique situation and is the ground of his anxiety: 'Anxiety is the inevitable concomitant of the paradox of freedom and finiteness in which man is involved,' says Niebuhr.

Man is unfinished but forever has the possibility of 'becoming'. By contrast the animals and plants, which appear frequently in Auden's poems as images of unawareness, are perfect, finished and for ever unpromising, unconscious of identity, of time and of choice:

> Let them leave language to their lonely betters
> Who count some days and long for certain letters;
> We, too, make noises when we laugh or weep,
> Words are for those with promises to keep.

and elsewhere,

> The hour-glass whispers to the lion's paw,
> The clock-towers tell the gardens day and night,
> How many errors time has patience for,
> How wrong they are in being always right.

So far this description might seem to suggest an anxiety-ridden outlook which could easily become querulous or nagging. Auden is never querulous and rarely nags; his purposiveness and sense of humour both relieve him. 'Accept the present in its fullness,' he says in a characteristically firm and positive passage. Man is a social creature, and a sign of the individual's growing spiritual maturity is the decision not to try one of the many forms of escape from this commitment, but to stay where he is, soberly and steadily to work out his destiny with the intransigent material of human relations. To work for *civility*, and to build the Just City—these are favourite phrases of Auden's. The building of the Just City can never be completed, he adds, but could not be even an aspiration were there not outside man an order of which his dream of the Just City is a reflection.

In all this, 'Love' is still often invoked by Auden, though now with a more complex sense of its difficulty and also of its ineluctability:

> O let none say I love until aware
> What huge resources it will take to nurse

One ruining speck, one tiny hair
That casts a shadow through the universe.

Auden's general approach is well illustrated in a vigorous and hortatory poem, 'Memorial for the City'. The theme is the destruction of traditional European values as they are expressed in the ancient city-architecture of the continent, and the now more plainly exposed dilemma of fallen man immersed in time:

The steady eyes of the crow and the camera's candid eye
See as honestly as they know how, but they lie.
The crime of life is not time. Even now, in this night
Among the ruins of the post-Vergilian city
Where our past is a chaos of graves and the barbed wire stretches
ahead
Into our future till it is lost to sight,
Our grief is not Greek: as we bury our dead
We know without knowing there is reason for what we bear,
That our hurt is a desertion, that we are to pity
Neither ourselves not our city;
Whoever the searchlights catch, whatever the loudspeakers
blare,
We are not to despair.

In a later poem, 'The Shield of Achilles', Thetis, the mother of Achilles, looks over the armourer Hephaestos's shoulder at the decorative scenes on the shield. Here is time and event, but without the sense of sin or the hope of redemption; a world which is, in the most terribly exact sense, meaningless:

A ragged urchin, aimless and alone,
Loitered about that vacancy, a bird
Flew up to safety from his well-aimed stone:
That girls are raped, that two boys knife a third,
Were axioms to him who'd never heard
Of any world where promises were kept.
Or one could weep because another wept.

The altered emphasis in Auden's preoccupations often brought with it a greater leanness and firmness of attitude. He seemed less attentive to the rich muddle of life. But we may be disproportionately fascinated, as well as seriously concerned, with the sheer detail of experience. In some ways

Auden's approach in the forties and early fifties was more austere than it used to be, closer to the kind of promise made in his earlier poems. And in seeking to express this new pattern of interests Auden developed some sinewy and complex verse of great power and interest.

(ii) *Symbolic Landscape and the Long Line*

For a few years after his arrival in America Auden apparently decided that he would, predominantly, write long poems (poems occupying all or most of one volume), whose structural complexities would embody a variety of materials, of tones and of intellectual approaches. Later his collections were of shorter poems, ranging from lyrics up to what might be called longish short poems (of from sixty to a hundred lines).

But between 1941 and 1948 Auden produced four long poems: *New Year Letter, The Sea and the Mirror, For the Time Being*, and *The Age of Anxiety*. Poetically, the first is the least interesting, though as we noted earlier. it has some moving lyric passages and is almost everywhere lively; and the Quest sonnets which complete the volume are more than good derivatives from Rilke. The title-poem draws to its close, all argument aside, with a joyful invocation to God:

> O Unicorn among the cedars,
> To whom no magic charm can lead us,
> White childhood moving like a sigh
> Through the green woods unharmed ...

The Sea and the Mirror is subtitled 'A Commentary on Shakespeare's *The Tempest*', and is chiefly about the relations between art, the artist and society. For each character Auden produces a different verse-form, often a highly elaborate one. The result is sometimes merely curious, though the performance is technically brilliant; and some parts (Alonso's address to Ferdinand; Miranda's *villanelle*), are not only brilliant but more deeply engaging.

For the Time Being, a Christmas oratorio dedicated to the memory of Auden's mother, is more emotionally harmonious than the other long poems, probably because of the greater simplicity and firmness of Auden's theme—of belief and hope, though in sin and humility. Here, not surprisingly, is to be found the peculiarly 'still' lyric note we remarked earlier:

Let number and weight rejoice
In this hour of their translation
Into conscious happiness
For the whole in every part,
The truth at the proper centre ...

The Age of Anxiety is brilliant, perverse, disjointed, a 'baroque eclogue' with all the extraneous ornamentation and deviousness that such a sub-title implies, a structural experiment that does not succeed. Yet even here, in a metre drawn from Anglo-Saxon verse, a few sections achieve an unusual gaunt beauty. A tired clerk in a New York bar nostalgically describes childhood in a city which might just as well have been Birmingham or Dortmund:

... how fagged coming home through
The urban evening. Heavy like us
Sank the gas-tanks—it was supper-time,
In hot houses helpless babies and
Telephones gabbled untidy cries,
And on embankments black with burnt grass
Shambling freight trains were shunted away
Past crimson clouds.

Perhaps in the last three of these long poems Auden was tackling his own form of a problem similar to that of T. S. Eliot in *The Waste Land* (though aspects of the same problem in its contemporary form can be seen at least as far back as Browning's *The Ring and the Book*): how to achieve a form which would embody the detail of social dilemmas, the diverse pressures of moral problems, and the necessary changes of tone, angle and level of suggestion—in a shape somehow organic to the theme. Auden does not succeed: *For the Time Being* is comparatively harmonious but not really complex; *The Sea and the Mirror* is complex and in a sense unified, but gains its unity chiefly from the assumed background of *The Tempest*.

In his shorter poems Auden continued to use several kinds of conversational metre, and seemed still to regard some of this verse as a sort of 'public' utterance, though now to a public accepted as small, and sympathetic by predisposition. This is an aspect of what Auden has called 'unofficial poetry' and 'comic' art:

> From now on the only popular art will be comic art—and this will be unpopular with the Management. It is the law which it cannot alter which is the subject of all comic art ... Every poet stands alone. [But] this does not mean that he sulks mysteriously in a corner by himself.

Cheerful and debunking comic art can help to preserve self-respect in increasingly 'generalized' societies. Against 'the lie of Authority' a poet, as one of the few individuals—by profession—in modern society, will oppose the idea of the personal life.

Auden seems to have a more deliberate and prescribed purpose in his later use of the conversational voice than he had earlier. He seems to be aiming not at a widely acceptable demotic speech but at a low-temperature verse of intelligent observation and comment:

> [We] would in the old grand manner
> Have sung from a resonant heart.
> But, pawed-at and gossiped-over
> By the promiscuous crowd,
> Concocted by editors
> Into spells to befuddle the crowd,
> All words like peace and love,
> All sane affirmative speech,
> Had been soiled, profaned, debased
> To a horrid mechanical screech:
> No civil style survived
> That pandemonium
> But the wry, the sotto-voce,
> Ironic and monochrome:

Verse such as this can induce its own cult-snobberies and is no doubt not meant to be of the first importance in the body of Auden's work. It is 'occasional' verse in a valid sense—verse written for and commenting on specific occasions—and within these limits it is usually acute and enjoyable. Inevitably, it retains some of the faults of its kind: it is sometimes slapdash and unmuscular, a versified *New*

Yorker journalese which may be observant and intelligent but is too brittle to cut deep.

In his imagery Auden turns instinctively to landscape: he commonly speaks of 'villages of the heart', 'our landscape of pain', 'suburbs of fear' and so on. We may say roughly that he has two distinctive kinds of natural imagery: that in which landscape is an illuminating backcloth to some human social activity, and that in which landscape is a symbol for an inner dilemma in human personality. Again speaking generally, we may say that the first predominates in Auden's earlier poetry, and the second later. Nowadays the great industrial cities of America may occasionally provide the first kind of imagery; and the Apennine backbone of Italy, dropping to its coastal plains, may provide the second. But the scenery common to the Northern and Midland Pennines of Auden's childhood and youth continued more than any other to be drawn on for both types of imagery. The lusher scenes of southern England—or the hollyhocks and lawns of Tennyson's rectory gardens—had little appeal for him.

In the thirties Auden was more likely than later to invoke the densely-packed, intensively worked-over, huddled and smoky Industrial Revolution landscapes of the Pennines, the grim and uncompromising little towns of the foothills and valleys or the great black sprawling cities on the plains below. He did write also of the bare stark uplands then, but was still likely to speak of them, with their abandoned workings and derelict mines, as illustrations of the same direct social interest; to use them, in short, as backcloths. And of course he loved them, and still loves them, in and for themselves:

Always my boy of wish returns
To those peat-stained deserted burns
That feed the Wear and Tyne and Tees.

During the fifties landscape became for Auden more and more a means of visually symbolizing the spiritual conflicts in man, and to this need the involved geometry of the upper hills speaks best. As in so much, Rilke had guided Auden to what he sought here:

One of the constant problems of the poet is how to express abstract ideas in concrete terms ... Rilke is almost the first poet since the seventeenth century to find a fresh solution ... [he] thinks of the human in terms of the non-human ... one of [his] most characteristic devices is the expression of human life in terms of landscape. It is this kind of imagery which is beginning to appear in English poetry.

Certainly Auden's use of landscape in the fifties expresses his characteristic urge to wrest meaningful patterns from experience. But it is important to recognize that the landscapes are not being wrenched into the form of symbols. They speak to him—had indeed always spoken to him, though not always receiving his later comprehension—as symbols, as 'sacred objects'. They spoke to him before he could consciously decipher their language:

... There
In Rookhope I was first aware;
Of Self and Not-Self, Death and Dread:
Audits were entrances which led
Down to the Outlawed, to the Others.
The Terrible, the Merciful, the Mothers;
Alone in the hot day I knelt
Upon the edge of shafts and felt
The deep *urmutterfurcht* that drives
Us into knowledge all our lives ...

The process is not a fitting of pictures to ideas, but is part of Auden's natural manner of establishing relations with the outside world, of establishing 'the relations of man—as a history-making person—to nature':

Whenever I begin to think
About the human creature we
Must nurse to sense and decency,
An English area comes to mind,
I see the native of my kind
As a locality I love ...

After the war Auden exercised this interest in symbolic landscape much more closely, especially in what were described earlier as longish short poems. The sequence began notably, with a remarkable poem, 'In Praise of Limestone', and was continued in the seven 'Bucolics' in his book, *The*

Shield of Achilles (1955). The symbolic landscape and the long line which usually accompanies it combined to make one of the most important and exciting post-war developments in Auden's work.

Auden would muse before a large and varied landscape and seek to evoke from within it his sense that it symbolized an extensive pattern of human dilemmas. In the following passage the people who remain within the gregarious life of the valleys are contrasted with the exceptional few who go elsewhere:

Adjusted to the local needs of valleys
Where everything can be touched or reached by walking,
Their eyes have never looked into infinite space
. . .

That is why, I suppose,
The best and worst never stayed here long but sought
Immoderate soils where the beauty was not so external,
The light less public and the meaning of life
Something more than a mad camp. 'Come!' cried the granite wastes,
'How evasive is your humour, how accidental
Your kindest kiss, how permanent is death.' (Saints-to-be
Slipped away sighing.) 'Come!' purred the clays and gravels.
'On our plains there is room for armies to drill; rivers
Wait to be tamed and slaves to construct you a tomb
In the grand manner; soft as the earth is mankind and both
Need to be altered.' (Intendant Caesars rose and
Left, slamming the door.) But the really reckless were fetched
By an older colder voice, the oceanic whisper:
'I am the solitude that asks and promises nothing;
That is how I shall set you free. There is no love;
There are only the various envies, all of them sad.'

Here Auden is using his long line and verse-sentence, which have themselves some of the qualities of his second kind of landscape. The lines are syllabically-counted (13 : 11 syllables, with elision of all contiguous vowels and through 'h'). They have a sinuous, following-through, flexible though connected movement; they follow the ideas suggested by the panorama, varying pitch easily as Auden turns to a new aspect or alters his angle of approach or branches into a side-consideration. They hold always to the main thread of the thought, though directed from moment to moment by its sinuosities and qualifications.

The intention differs from that which produced the curt epigrammatic line of the mid-thirties and probably owes most, in so far as it is indebted to Auden's earlier practice, to the conversational verse of the later thirties. The long verse-sentence is unusually free from the more obvious demands of line-endings (as, for instance, Auden's laconic sonnets necessarily were not). It is less immediately restricting than the three or four iambic line of Yeats—though that line was so magnificently varied in Yeats's hands that its apparent limitations turned to real advantage. Auden, we know, immensely admired the Yeatsian line and had sometimes used it. But a longer and more loosely-articulated line seemed more natural to him.

Like most of even the valuable developments in Auden's verse this line is frequently marred—in this case by jarring and artistically unjustified changes of tone and attitude, and especially by a tiresome over-insistence on remaining unbuttoned. We see the point, in the passage quoted above, about 'Intendant Caesars ... slamming the door' (it echoes an assertion by Joseph Goebbels), but the combination is intellectually pert. On the other hand, the verb 'fetched' in the same line has a nice ambiguity, drawn from Auden's acquaintance with contemporary American vernacular. To most English readers the verb will mean 'brought' or 'called away'; to an American it is likely to mean also 'emotionally bowled over' (as when jazz enthusiasts say that a solo performer 'fetches' them). And this second association—of something slightly hysteric—does add to the ironic texture of the passage.

At its best the long verse-sentence has a beautifully easy spoken note, an attractive mixture of colloquialism and serious observation, of wit and of moral concern—all managed with a verbal and aural skill which hardly any other living poet can approach. The shape and movement of the poem acts out, as it were, the tense dialectic of the poet's will, mind and heart. In the following passage Auden opens on a typical landscape, limestone hills above the wide plains and their towns. The landscape is both actually and symbolically moving to him:

If it form the one landscape that we the inconstant ones
  Are consistently homesick for, this is chiefly
Because it dissolves in water. Mark these rounded slopes
  With their surface fragrance of thyme and beneath
A secret system of caves and conduits; hear these springs
  That spurt out everywhere with a chuckle
Each filling a private pool for its fish and carving
  Its own little ravine whose cliffs entertain
The butterfly and the lizard; examine this region
  Of short distances and definite places ...

So the complex interplay of human motives for which this landscape speaks begins to be developed. The poem closes on a view in perspective of the statues man makes out of this same rock, and farther back—picking up again the wider panoramic view of the opening—of the rock in its aboriginal landscape:

... In so far as we have to look forward
  To death as a fact, no doubt we are right: But if
Sins can be forgiven, if bodies rise from the dead,
  These modifications of matter into
Innocent athletes and gesticulating fountains,
  Made solely for pleasure, make a further point:
The blessed will not care what angle they are regarded from,
  Having nothing to hide. Dear, I know nothing of
Either, but when I try to imagine a faultless love
  Or the life to come, what I hear is the murmur
Of underground streams, what I see is a limestone landscape.

This kind of poetic activity is altogether less gregarious and less intellectually extensive than that normally associated with Auden's work in the thirties. But it emerged naturally from the broad lines of his intellectual and poetic development up to that point.

IV. FROM THE MID-FIFTIES TO 1973

Lost of course and myself owing a death

(i) *Divided Aims: The Game of Knowledge*

Can I learn to suffer
Without saying something ironic or funny
On suffering?

Auden's work after the war, especially up to *Homage to Clio* (1960), expresses some striking tensions and divisions; expresses them with unusual directness. The tensions seem to be of three main kinds, each a matter of uncertain relationships: between Auden and his audience, between the artist and the moralizer; and between the artist and the believer.

We noted earlier that Auden was at that time somewhat more 'austere' and less 'knowing' than he used to be. But the difference is one of degree. He was still very often unsteady in tone and taste; the excellent parts have still to be sifted from much that is merely clever-clever or spry (a poem such as 'Homage to Clio' shows this as well as any). To say this is not to be academically portentous or to forget that, now as always, a part of Auden's pertness arises from a deliberate wish to flout all conceptions of artistic decorum. This particular quality is not a tough or quirky comedy so much as something would-be funny. Several kinds of instance could be cited: the raiding of the dictionary for words which are not merely odd but unhelpfully odd; the overworking of pat endings which had persisted since the early sonnets; the drop into an affectedly colloquial manner; the showy manipulation of conceits; in short, a recurrent bright technical flurry.

These faults seem to arise in part from Auden's unsureness about his exact audience, his lack of relation to a known and fairly homogeneous group whose attitudes he habitually appreciated. He had, we know, a considerable capacity for friendship; and he was not without a good circle of admirers among poets—indeed, he has been a strong influence on American poetry for many years. He was yet in one sense isolated, and this is partly the result of the move we discussed earlier and sought to justify.

We do not now retract that justification. But we need to see as sharply as possible the problems it presented Auden. The difficulty of knowing just to whom he was speaking had sometimes led him to solitary verbal pirouettes or to new versions of the 'private joking in panelled rooms' of which he accused himself in the thirties. At such times the audience seems to be either a very small 'in-group', or almost hypothetical—the audience of the brighter weeklies, say, which is not really any of us but is parts of many of us on both sides of the Atlantic, and which is intellectually fashionable.

But occasionally Auden could speak steadily as well as wittily and intelligently to an audience composed, we may imagine, of what he called 'ironic points of light'; of people whose irony does not preclude charity, who are interested in both poetry and moral ideas, who are on the whole unambitious and who try to steer honestly between righteous indignation, contempt and self-surrender. No doubt this is a small audience, scattered and hard to find. But it exists, and Auden's career particularly qualified him to seek it:

> O every day in sleep and labour
> Our life and death are with our neighbour,
> And love illuminates again
> The city and the lion's den
> The world's great rage, the travel of young men.

In his vividly metaphorical, alert and companionable conversational verse and in his landscape poetry Auden could sometimes reach out to the kinds of audience he might particularly address. 'In Praise of Limestone' is a fine poem and yet a poem severed from local cultures. Its unrooted, engaged intelligence sees, and sees through, the landscape. The later 'Whitsunday in Kirchstetten', to which we will return, rediscovers the sense of locality, and is companionable in a way which recalls some of the poems of friendship in the early thirties (such as 'Out on the lawn I lie in bed') but is less parochial.

Auden's second area of tension lies in the uneasy relationship between the purposive moralist and the creative artist—the artist who is not concerned to wrest statements from experience directly but works in the intuitive knowledge that, to use Yeats's phrase, 'words alone are certain good'. We have referred to an aspect of this much earlier. Since Auden now sees the problem more clearly, the split is not so sharp-edged. It is still there, as the disconcerting unevenness of such a poem as 'Memorial for the City' shows. Auden simply will not leave the good verse of the poem's first section to work in its own way, but continues by piling up bright *aperçus*. He is able to quote with obvious approval, 'the value of art lies in its effects—not in beauty but in right action'; but he can also refer to 'the devil's subtlest temptation, the desire to do good by [your] art'. There need be no real contradiction there. Yet for a personality such as Auden's there is likely to be a powerful tension until the exact ways in which each statement may be true have been resolved.

The work of resolution leads directly into what we are calling Auden's third problem. Around this whole area he exercised his mind considerably for many years, and it was entirely typical that he should have devoted his Inaugural Lecture as Professor of Poetry at Oxford to aspects of it. The core of the question is the relation of the poet and his work to himself as a man (fallen, free, bound and wilful) and so to God. Its main divisions are: what are the dangers of artistic vocation? What are the justifications?

The theme of the spiritual dangers in the life of an artist has engaged several important contemporary writers, notably Eliot and Mann. There are striking similarities between the theme of Mann's story *Death in Venice* and the long second part of Caliban's vivid parody of the later Henry James (and also in the whole concept of Prospero) in *The Sea and the Mirror*. If man's life is a constant struggle in the will, how far is the artist tempted—because he is a sort of creator—to abrogate this responsibility? to get, so to speak, between himself and God? 'The artist up to his old game of playing at God with words', quotes Auden from Kierkegaard, and adds a note from the same source about the need to 'get out of the poetical into the existential'.

Auden had, therefore, to define to his own satisfaction the justification of art. His most typical single phrase from many on the subject asserts that poetry is 'a game of knowledge'. First, poetry (and all art) is a *game*. It is a form of magic (the naming of 'sacred objects') and of fun ('the joke of rhyme'), a release for writer and reader, inspired first not by a desire to do good or acquire fame but by a love of 'playing around with words'. Also as a game, it is not finally real or serious as 'theology and horses' are; it 'makes nothing happen'. Again like a game, it has fixed rules (patterns, rituals, ceremonies, forms, 'necessities') which the players must obey if they are to enjoy. But also pure luck ('the luck of verbal playing') has a part; something is simply 'given' (grace?). 'Only your song is an absolute gift,' Auden says of the composer, and intends the line to carry the ambiguities of both the idiomatic and the philosophic meanings. The practice of art was for Auden yet another example of the fruitful paradox of freedom and necessity.

Yet poetry is a game of *knowledge*. It is in a certain sense concerned with knowledge, and its magic is meaningful. The knowledge is, though, a product of the play and comes by indirection, as in the serious absorbed play of a child. Aesthetic patterns and resolutions are not metaphysical patterns and resolutions ('Analogy is not identity'), but can analogously point towards them: 'And the hard bright light composes / A meaningless moment into an eternal fact.' In art's harmony and ritual are mirrored the possibility of a greater order outside man's power; both demand 'an acknowledgement that there are relationships which are obligatory and independent of our personality'.

So poetry can help to 'direct us to ourselves', can 'persuade' us to a form of 'moral rejoicing', can point through man's 'lying nature' to 'love and truth'. At this stage this was the fullest expression of Auden's continuing urge to irradiate daily human activity with mythical meaning and of his questioning of the relation between art and moral purpose. By the sixties the dilemma was still not altogether resolved in Auden's personality and could create a jarring unsteadiness. To regret this unsteadiness is not to make aesthetic considerations override all others. For we may say that to the artist, in a special sense, 'analogy *must be* identity', that the tense play of ambiguities which make up a poem is indeed part of the poet's 'being'.

(ii) *Prose*

Of all Auden's varied output during the last dozen years of his life, two main elements demand to be discussed in particular: his prose criticism and his four final volumes of verse (one of them posthumous).

Actually, the earliest volume of prose criticism, *The Enchafèd Flood*, dates back to 1951. It is still interesting and indeed exciting to read; and it showed what were to be over the following twenty or so years the main characteristics of Auden's considerable prose output: his literary criticism is freely-ranging, synoptic, paradoxical, aphoristic. It is not much concerned (though it can be occasionally) with close critical analysis of the words on the page; it is much more likely to muse widely on the symbolic and philosophic implications of a work, to deal in parables, recurrent themes, archetypes, myths, patterns.

The Enchafèd Flood, which began as a named series of lectures for the University of Virginia, is thus closely organized around a number of related themes, those of the romantic symbolism of the sea and of the desert. These were issues to which Auden returned again and again, notably in *The Sea and the Mirror* (1945), *The Age of Anxiety* (1948), the 'Bucolics' (1955) and other landscape poems. He made use of a similar general approach when he delivered the 1967 T. S. Eliot Memorial Lectures in the University of Kent at Canterbury, which were subsequently published as *Secondary Worlds* (1968). Primary worlds are those of everyday social experience; secondary worlds are those of art: the phrases themselves are from his beloved Tolkien. Here is a typical quotation, typical not only of his manner but of one of his recurrent themes, an aspect of the relations between art and life:

> All art is gratuitous [a favourite word], so that one can never say that a certain kind of society must necessarily produce a certain kind of art. On the other hand, when we consider a certain society and the literature which it did actually produce, we can sometimes see reasons why it was possible for such a society to produce it.

Outside these two 'commissioned' volumes, Auden wrote essay after essay for all sorts of different occasions but especially as introductions to collections of other men's work, as long reviews and as lectures. His poetry cannot usefully be described as 'literary'; there are manifestly literary elements, but they are not a major part of the poems' qualities. But he was certainly a very literary and scholarly man, and the overall impression created by his great bulk of essays is the pendulum swing from literary and historical allusion to general analysis and observation on almost any subject under the sun. The fruit of all this effort, covering about thirty years, is to be found in the more than five-hundred pages each of *The Dyer's Hand* (1963) and *Forewords and Afterwords* (1973).

Here we can see in full measure Auden's main qualities as a critic and indeed as a personality, since his own style comes out, necessarily, more directly in his prose than in his poetry. He has a whole range of favourite themes and favourite approaches, ways of dealing with those themes. He also has certain favourite single notions, mild bees in his bonnet: such as the impropriety of publishing a man's letters after his death, or the virtues and the limits of English family life (really, of English upper middle-class professional family life in the first three or four decades of this century. He never ceased, in spite of all his criticisms, to feel both a nostalgia and a moral admiration for that).

Of his major recurrent themes, one of the two or three most dominant is, once again, the relations between art and life. He talks, at different points in these two volumes, about poems as belonging to a 'limitless world of pure joy', about art as 'a mirror in which [we] may become conscious of what [our] own feelings really are; its proper effect, in fact, is disenchanting', about poetry as 'a clarification of life' and concerned with two key questions 'Who am I?' and 'Whom ought I to become?', and about a poem as 'a dialectical struggle between the events the poet wishes to embody and the verbal system'. A hundred other similar quotations could have been brought forward.

Or one recalls Auden's fondness for observing animals and then for teasing out reflections on the human condition by comparing man ... self-aware, having free will, using language ... with animals or birds which have none of these things. Robert Bloom, an American critic, is surely right to call the two essays collected as 'Two Bestiaries' in *The Dyer's Hand*, and devoted respectively to D. H. Lawrence and Marianne Moore, 'masterful, learned and penetrating' and to go on to relate them to Auden's own animal poems: 'in them, Auden manifests his own affection for humankind, and his sacred sense of its transcendence over the creatures. And his urgent concern with the nature and exigencies of the human predicament has from the beginning of his career testified to his unending preoccupation with the Good Life.'

Yet again, these essays illustrate time after time the perceptiveness, the unusualness, often the quixotry of Auden's powers of general observation. Read only the essay in *The Dyer's Hand* called 'The American Scene' which embodies an exceptional range of insights on the texture and nature of American life. Or note the incidental comments scattered throughout his essays, such as this one:

> In any modern city, a great deal of our energy has to be expended in *not* seeing, *not* hearing, *not* smelling. An inhabitant of New York who possessed the sensory acuteness of an African Bushman would very soon go mad.

And here is a remarkably percipient short paragraph on Rudyard Kipling:

> His poems in their quantity, their limitation to one feeling at a time, have the air of brilliant tactical improvisations to overcome sudden unforeseen obstacles, as if, for Kipling, experience were not a seed to cultivate patiently and lovingly, but an unending stream of dangerous feelings to be immediately mastered as they appear.

These two volumes show also, once again and time after time, Auden's love of myth, structure, pattern. I am not myself a reader or a lover of the 'detective story', that characteristically English form of fiction (which is to be distinguished from the gangster novel, the spy thriller or the *roman policier*). It was bound to appeal to Auden, and his essay on the genre is, even for one who does not read them, a fascinating exercise in elaborate pattern-tracing and symbol-identification. Auden never tired of this kind of exercise; here he is in the course of an essay on Grimm and Andersen:

> A fairy story, as distinct from a merry tale, or an animal story, is a serious tale with a human hero and a happy ending. The

progression of its hero is the reverse of the tragic hero's: at the beginning he is either socially obscure or despised as being stupid or untalented, lacking in the heroic virtues, but at the end, he has surprised everyone by demonstrating his heroism and winning fame, riches and love.

Or consider the perfectly typical opening of *Secondary Worlds*:

> In myth, history and literature, we meet four kinds of human beings, of whom it may be said that their deaths are the most significant event in their lives, the Sacrificial Victim, the Epic Hero, the Tragic Hero and the Martyr.

He then proceeds to define them one by one before beginning to play variations on the concepts. Auden's essays, for all their occasional prejudices, opinionations and admonishings, are on the whole a source of continuous pleasure and insight—into both literature and experience.

(iii) *Poetry and Companionability*

Auden's poetry of the sixties and seventies is on the whole more closely contained, more quietly ruminative than before. Technically it is as brilliant as ever, inventive, witty and extraordinarily skilful. But there is little larger formal experiment. The predominant tones and manners are occasional, domestic, relaxed and idiomatic rather than more largely thematic or outward-turned.

In the light of all this we can make new glosses on the three divisions in Auden's work which we discussed earlier. As for the relation between Auden and his audience: the audience envisaged in this last period is, more often than not, a small group of good friends. Sometimes there is even—though partly with the tongue in the cheek—a prim, keep-your-distance manner towards outsiders. Catching familiar notes in these late poems one realizes sharply that much of Auden's poetry right from the beginning addressed itself to, found its voice in, a small, known, domestic group of friends. It seems, at first glance, ironic that Auden's reputation in the thirties should have been so much that of 'the conscience of his generation', which seems to imply adopting a much more public intellectual stance. But the reputation was fairly gained; at bottom there is no real contradiction between the two claims.

In talking about the tension between the artist and the moralist in Auden we discussed his description of poetry as 'a game of knowledge'. The stress later, both in his criticism and in his poetry, was less on the 'knowledge' and more on the 'game', more on poetry as verbal artifice expressing celebration, awe or piety before experience. Third, the tension between the artist and the believer seemed less, because poetry had been put in its place as, in the last resort, a side-occupation or exercise. Enormously worthwhile, of course:

> ... After all, it's rather a privilege
> amid the affluent traffic
> to serve this unpopular art

but still, as the tone of the above quotation conveys, a marginal matter, secondary to the real questions of faith and the effort to serve God. That life, too, does not demand melodramatic, rhetorical or histrionic responses. Best, without underestimating the actual melodrama of experience, to work quietly and as well as one can; where we are, trusting in God and his grace. The times may tempt us to do otherwise, and especially tempt writers to assume roles beyond their competence; these voices have to be quietly ignored.

Hence, Auden's last four volumes of verse, which cover the final dozen years of his life, show—like his prose—certain strongly marked and distinctive qualities. The volumes are *About the House* (1966), *City without Walls* (1969), *Epistle to a Godson* (1972) and the posthumous *Thank You, Fog* (1974). They have common qualities of theme and tone which mark them off fairly decisively from the volumes which preceded them.

It is useful to read them also in conjunction with his commonplace book, *A Certain World* (1971) which, through deploying his favourite extracts from a multitude of writers of many times and nationalities, shows well once again the strange conformations of his idiosyncratic mind. The book is, he said, not an autobiography (he would never have written one of those) but 'a map of my planet'. Here, too, are all his favourite ideas, but put by other men: that poetry makes nothing happen, that it is a form of pure play, that listening to the birds reminds you that man is a creature with 'the right to make promises', or—as Hazlitt is quoted as saying—'man is the only animal that laughs and weeps', that man is haunted by the difference between what is and what might have been, the exerciser of free will, choice, commitments in speech; and so on.

In these last four volumes of poetry, in general, Auden writes less than he used to about political or public matters and much more about personal. It still largely lacks the kind of intimacy whose absence from his poetry, throughout his career, I noted earlier. But this later poetry is much more about personal matters, which is why I used the word 'companionability' in the title to this section. I think it is fair to say that most critics do not think as highly of these later volumes as of the earlier. I do, and find they give a valuable new dimension to the body of Auden's work.

It is poetry of, first, acceptance; acceptance of creatureliness, of the real world (under God), of the temporal order. It is a poetry of celebration of that natural world and of harmony and measure before it; it is a humane poetry. One characteristic tone, and some of its basic seriousness, are caught in the last lines of the last poem of *About the House*:

> ... about
> catastrophe or how to behave in one
> I know nothing, except what everyone knows—
> if there when Grace dances, I should dance.

It is therefore a poetry which pivots around the idea of a modest, unarrogant acceptance of the self—'my personal city'—and of the body, of home (there are many poems of 'place') and of friendship. Here we need to say more about the rôle of that small group of friends to which I referred earlier. Look only at the dedications of many of these later poems; they are to living friends, *in memoriam* for dead friends, to doctors, the local priest (in Austria), relatives, a godchild. It is a small group and the sense of it was intensified by Auden's renewed Oxford links; the pull of all that held.

All this is admirable, and we should try to take it straight and link it with Auden's continuing preoccupations; in both small and large senses he was coming home. By 'small' senses I mean that this poetry could occasionally be that of a rather stiff, mandarin, Oxford man who knew he had been to the best place and who, with his friends, never quite got rid of a sense that the great body of people outside were not quite as nice as *they* were. But then Auden was always very conscious of his privacy and inviolability. He has a right to be like that. What seems to me less justifiable is the tampering with the chronology of the poetry so as to put people off tracing any lines of development (he later allowed chronological printing) and, even more, amending poems written many years ago. Auden justified this by saying:

I have never, consciously at any rate, attempted to revise my former thoughts or feelings, only the language in which they were first expressed when, on further consideration, it seemed to me inaccurate, lifeless, prolix or painful to the ear.

I do not think that the full range of his later amendments is caught within the above prescription; some of them do indicate revisions of thoughts and feelings.

The tone is almost always low-keyed (and sometimes High Camp). There are irritating oddities and pawkinesses, but overall I would agree with Replogle that throughout this last period Auden can be called almost exclusively a comic poet and that he wrote some of his best poems in this mode. At their best these are seriously playful poems, domestic, conversational, both warm and dry.

As to their craft they are, to use a favourite word of Auden himself in this connexion, elegant 'contraptions'. They tend to build up a labyrinthine and complex interplay of tones and meanings so that Johnson, in a particularly subtle book on Auden's poetry—*Man's Place*—can speak of 'the coherence of idea, art, organization and tone' in these later poems.

We noted earlier that after the late forties Auden wrote no more very long poems. But what may be said to have taken their place, and he wrote them for more than a decade thereafter, were linked groups, series or sequences of poems; again I would agree with Johnson that these are among his most substantial achievements. They include, in *The Shield of Achilles* (1955), the seven 'Bucolics', a further development of that landscape poetry to which we have referred earlier, and the seven 'Horae Canonicae' in the same volume, a superb sequence. Then, in *About the House* (1966) there were the twelve poems called 'Thanksgiving for a Habitat' which are capped, in the same volume, by the fluently tender 'Whitsunday in Kirchstetten' from whose last lines I quoted a little earlier in this section. Finally, there are the eight songs from 'Mother Courage' in *City Without Walls* (1969).

The harvest of these last years, in short, was a very good and a distinctive one; without it English poetry—and our understanding of Auden's own capacities as a poet—would have been the poorer.

Consistently, through more than forty years of writing, Auden rejected 'the soft carpets and big desks' of the successful men-of-letters and stuck to his explorations with a quite unusual devotion. He made his own mistakes in his own way and, by example and precept, urged 'the acceptance by every individual of his aloneness and his responsibility for it, and a willingness continually to re-examine his assumptions'. We have suggested that in one sense poetry seemed less absorbing to Auden in his last decade than heretofore. Yet still poetry remained his natural way of speaking; he was always a dedicated poet for whom the practice of poetry was an activity of the moral will. He pursued his honestly persistent inquiries eagerly and hopefully. He could write:

> ... wherever
> The sun shines, brooks run, books are written
> There will also be this death ...

But also, just as characteristically, he wrote:

> After so many years the light is
> Novel still and immensely ambitious.

Meanwhile, Auden's achievement is remarkable: in much pithily epigrammatic verse; in many lovely songs, lyrics and sonnets; in a flexible, acute and often comic conversational verse and in his moral-landscape poetry. He helped considerably to define and make articulate our situation in the thirties, and also in the fifties, as this finely rhetorical passage from 'The Shield of Achilles' will remind us:

> The mass and majesty of this world, all
> That carries weight and always weighs the same
> Lay in the hands of others; they were small
> And could not hope for help and no help came:
> What their foes liked to do was done, their shame
> Was all the worst could wish; they lost their pride
> And died as men before their bodies died.

Later, the sense of dramatic menace receded and with it some kinds of urgency in Auden's verse. He now sought different music, other relationships; and in doing so he went back more than ever to his origins:

> Let your last thinks all be thanks:
> praise your parents who gave you
> a Super-ego of strength
> that saves you so much bother
> digit friends and dear them all,
> then pay fair attribution
> to your age, to having been
> born when you were. In boyhood
> you were permitted to meet
> beautiful old contraptions ...

Of all this, the result is a considerable body of memorable speech on our times and problems, an example which contributes to the *civility* Auden so much admired, and a commitment which claims our respect and admiration.

W. H. AUDEN

A Select Bibliography

(Place of publication London, unless stated otherwise)

Bibliography:

'A W. H. Auden Bibliography, 1924–55', compiled by J. P. Clancy, *Thought* (Fordham University), xxx, Summer 1955.

AN ANNOTATED CHECK LIST OF THE WORKS OF W. H. AUDEN, by E. Callan; Denver (1958).

W. H. AUDEN, A BIBLIOGRAPHY: The Early years through 1955, by B. C. Bloomfield; Charlottesville, Va. (1964)

—2nd ed. by B. C. Bloomfield and Edward Mendelson, 1972, extends the bibliography, 1924–1969.

Separate Works and Collections:

POEMS (1930)

—includes *Paid on Both Sides*, a charade in verse. Rev. edition, 1933.

THE ORATORS: An English study (1932). *Verse and Prose*

—rev. editions, 1934 and 1966. The 1966 edition includes a preface by the author.

THE DANCE OF DEATH (1933). *Charade (verse and prose)*

THE DOG BENEATH THE SKIN, OR, WHERE IS FRANCIS? (1935). *Drama (verse and prose)*

—in collaboration with Christopher Isherwood.

LOOK, STRANGER! (1936). *Verse*

—published in the USA under the title *On the Island*, 1937.

THE ASCENT OF F6 (1936). *Drama (verse and prose)*

—in collaboration with Christopher Isherwood. Rev. edition, 1937.

SPAIN (1937). *Verse*

—a pamphlet poem.

LETTERS FROM ICELAND (1937). *Travel (verse and prose)*

—in collaboration with Louis MacNeice.

ON THE FRONTIER (1938). *Drama (verse and prose)*

—in collaboration with Christopher Isherwood.

SELECTED POEMS (1938).

JOURNEY TO A WAR (1939). *Travel*

—in collaboration with Christopher Isherwood. Includes the sonnet sequence 'In Time of War' (by W. H. Auden). Rev. edition, 1973.

SOME POEMS (1940)

—a small selection of previously published verse.

ANOTHER TIME (1940). *Verse*

NEW YEAR LETTER (1941). *Verse*

—published in the same year in the USA under the title *The Double Man*. Includes the long title poem, the sonnet sequence 'The Quest' and a prologue and epilogue.

THREE SONGS FOR ST CECILIA'S DAY (1941)

—privately printed.

FOR THE TIME BEING (1945). *Verse*

—contains also *The Sea and the Mirror:* a Commentary on Shakespeare's *The Tempest.*

THE AGE OF ANXIETY: A Baroque eclogue (1948). *Verse*

COLLECTED SHORTER POEMS, 1930–1944 (1950).

THE ENCHAFÈD FLOOD, OR, THE ROMANTIC ICONOGRAPHY OF THE SEA (1951). *Criticism*

—the Page-Barbour Lectures, University of Virginia, 1949.

NONES (1952). *Verse*

MOUNTAINS (1954). *Verse*

—a Faber Ariel poem.

THE SHIELD OF ACHILLES (1955). *Verse*

THE OLD MAN'S ROAD; New York (1956). *Verse*

W. H. AUDEN: A Selection by the author (1958). *Verse*

HOMAGE TO CLIO (1960). *Verse*

THE DYER'S HAND AND OTHER ESSAYS (1963). *Criticism*

SELECTED ESSAYS (1964). *Criticism*

ABOUT THE HOUSE (1966). *Verse*

COLLECTED SHORTER POEMS, 1927–1957 (1966).

COLLECTED LONGER POEMS (1968).

SECONDARY WORLDS (1968). *Criticism*

—the T. S. Eliot memorial lectures at the University of Kent, 1967.

CITY WITHOUT WALLS AND OTHER POEMS (1969). *Verse*

ACADEMIC GRAFFITI (1971). *Light verse*

EPISTLE TO A GODSON AND OTHER POEMS (1972). *Verse*

FOREWORDS AND AFTERWORDS, selected by Edward Mendelson (1973). *Criticism*

THANK YOU FOG: Last Poems (1974). *Verse*

COLLECTED POEMS (1976).

Libretti, etc.:

NO MORE PEACE: A THOUGHTFUL COMEDY, by E. Toller, translated by E. Crankshaw (1937)

—lyrics translated and adapted by W. H. Auden.

THE RAKE'S PROGRESS—an opera. Music by I. Stravinsky, libretto by W. H. Auden and Chester Kallman (1951).

THE MAGIC FLUTE—an opera in Two Acts with a new English libretto by W. H. Auden and Chester Kallman (1957).

ELEGY FOR YOUNG LOVERS—an opera. Libretto by W. H. Auden and Chester Kallmann; Mainz (1961).

THE BASSARIDS. Libretto by W. H. Auden and Chester Kallman (1966)
—performed at Salzburg.

LOVE'S LABOUR'S LOST. Libretto by W. H. Auden and Chester Kallman (1973)
—performed in Brussels.

PAUL BUNYAN—Operetta. Music by B. Britten, libretto by W. H. Auden (1976)
—performed at Columbia University in May 1941.

Edited Works, Introductions, Translations and Collections:

OXFORD POETRY (1926). *Anthology*
—in collaboration with C. Plumb.

OXFORD POETRY (1927). *Anthology*
—in collaboration with C. Day Lewis.

THE POET'S TONGUE (1935). *Anthology*
—in collaboration with J. Garrett.

Poetry (Chicago), XLIX, January 1937
—in collaboration with M. Roberts.

THE OXFORD BOOK OF LIGHT VERSE (1938). *Anthology*

THE AMERICAN SCENE, by Henry James. Introductory essay by W. H. Auden; New York (1946)
—the introduction was reprinted in *Horizon*, No. 86, Feb. 1947.

TENNYSON (1946)
—a selection from his poems with an introduction.

SLICK BUT NOT STREAMLINED, by John Betjeman; New York (1947)
—poems and short pieces selected and introduced by W. H. Auden.

THE PORTABLE GREEK READER; New York (1948)
—introduction by W. H. Auden.

INTIMATE JOURNALS, by Baudelaire, translated by C. Isherwood and introduced by W. H. Auden (1949).

SELECTED PROSE AND POETRY OF POE, ed. and introduced by W. H. Auden; New York (1950).

POETS OF THE ENGLISH LANGUAGE, 5 vols (1952). *Anthology*
—in collaboration with N. H. Pearson.

KIERKEGAARD, selected and introduced by W. H. Auden (1955).

THE FABER BOOK OF MODERN AMERICAN VERSE (1956). *Anthology*

THE SELECTED WRITINGS OF SIDNEY SMITH (1957).

AN ELIZABETHAN SONG BOOK, ed. W. H. Auden and Chester Kallman; New York (1955)
—music edited by N. Greenberg, 1957.

THE COMPLETE POEMS OF CAVAFY, translated by R. Dalvin and introduced by W. H. Auden; New York (1961).

GOETHE: ITALIAN JOURNEY, 1786–1788, translated and introduced by W. H. Auden and Elizabeth Mayer (1962).

A CHOICE OF DE LA MARE'S VERSE, selected with an introduction by W. H. Auden (1963).

MARKINGS, by Dag Hammarskjold and Leif Sjöberg, with a foreword by W. H. Auden (1964).

THE FABER BOOK OF APHORISMS: A Personal selection, by W. H. Auden and Louis Kronenberger (1964).

NINETEENTH-CENTURY MINOR POETS, ed. W. H. Auden (1966).

THE ELDER EDDA: A Selection, translated from the Icelandic by Paul B. Taylor and W. H. Auden (1969).

G. K. CHESTERTON: A Selection from his non-fictional prose, selected by W. H. Auden (1970).

A CERTAIN WORLD: A Commonplace book (1971). *Anthology*

SELECTED POEMS OF GUNNAR EKELÖF, translated by W. H. Auden and Leif Sjöberg (1971).

A CHOICE OF DRYDEN'S VERSE, selected and with an introduction by W. H. Auden (1973).

GEORGE HERBERT, selected by W. H. Auden (1973).

EVENING LAND, by Pär Lagerkvist, translated by W. H. Auden and Leif Sjöberg (1977).

Some Critical and Biographical Studies:

NEW BEARINGS IN ENGLISH POETRY, by F. R. Leavis (1932).

THE DESTRUCTIVE ELEMENT, by Stephen Spender (1935)
—Part 3 is relevant.

THE FABER BOOK OF MODERN VERSE, ed. M. Roberts (1936)
—new ed., 1951.

*ENEMIES OF PROMISE, by C. Connolly (1938).

*LIONS AND SHADOWS, by C. Isherwood (1938).

MODERN POETRY: A Personal essay, by Louis MacNeice (1938).

MODERN POETRY AND THE TRADITION, by C. Brooks; Chapel Hill (1939).

THE PRESENT AGE FROM 1914, by E. Muir (1939)
—a useful background handbook. Brought up to 1950 with new survey by D. Daiches, 1957.

DIRECTIONS IN MODERN POETRY, by E. Drew; New York (1940).

SOWING THE SPRING, by J. G. Southworth; Oxford (1940)
—a study devoted exclusively to the 'Auden Group'.

'Changes of Attitude and Rhetoric in Auden's Poetry', by R. Jarrell, *Southern Review*, VII, 1941.

AUDEN AND AFTER, by F. Scarfe (1942).

LIFE AND THE POET, by Stephen Spender (1942).

THE PERSONAL PRINCIPLE, by D. S. Savage (1944).

'Freud To Paul. The Stages of Auden's Ideology', by R. Jarrell, *Partisan Review*, XII, 1945.

POETRY OF THE PRESENT, ed. G. Grigson (1949)
—the introduction to this anthology is particularly valuable.

AUDEN, by F. Scarfe; Monaco (1949).

THE TELL-TALE ARTICLE, by G. Rostrevor Hamilton (1949).

AUDEN: AN INTRODUCTORY ESSAY, by R. Hoggart (1951).

*WORLD WITHIN A WORLD, by Stephen Spender (1951).

THE MODERN WRITER AND HIS WORLD, by G. S. Fraser (1953)
—rev. edition, 1964.

MORE MODERN AMERICAN POETS, by J. G. Southworth (1954).

PREDILECTIONS, by M. Moore; New York (1955).

*THE WHISPERING GALLERY, by J. Lehmann (1955).

THE MAKING OF THE AUDEN CANON, by J. W. Beach; Minnesota (1957).

THE ROMANTIC SURVIVAL, by J. Bayley (1957).

THE SHAPING SPIRIT, by A. Alvarez (1958).

VISION AND RHETORIC, by G. S. Fraser (1959).

W. H. AUDEN: A Selection, by R. Hoggart (1961).

THE POETRY OF W. H. AUDEN: The Disenchanted Island, by M. K. Spears; New York (1963).

AUDEN, by B. Everett (1964).

AUDEN: A Collection of critical essays, ed. M. K. Spears; Englewood Cliffs, New Jersey (1964).

THE POETIC ART OF W. H. AUDEN, by John G. Blair; Princeton (1965).

QUEST FOR THE NECESSARY: W. H. Auden and the Dilemma of Divided Consciousness, by Herbert Greenberg; Cambridge, Mass. (1968).

CHANGES OF HEART: A Study of the poetry of W. H. Auden, by Gerald Nelson (1969).

AUDEN'S POETRY, by Justin Replogle (1969).

W. H. AUDEN, by George T. Wright (1969).

THE LATER AUDEN, by George W. Bahlke; New Brunswick (1970).

W. H. AUDEN, by Dennis Davison (1970).

A READER'S GUIDE TO W. H. AUDEN, by John Fuller (1970).

W. H. AUDEN AS A SOCIAL POET, by Frederick Buell; Ithaca (1973).

MAN'S PLACE: An Essay on Auden, by Richard Johnson; Ithaca (1973).

W. H. AUDEN: A Tribute, ed. Stephen Spender (1975).

THE AUDEN GENERATION: Literature and Politics in England in the 1930s, by Samuel Hynes (1976).

*Autobiography, containing reminiscence and comment on W. H. Auden as a young man.

WRITERS AND THEIR WORK

General Surveys:

THE DETECTIVE STORY IN BRITAIN: Julian Symons
THE ENGLISH BIBLE: Donald Coggan
ENGLISH MARITIME WRITING: Hakluyt to Cook: Oliver Warner
THE ENGLISH SHORT STORY: I & II: T. O. Beachcroft
THE ENGLISH SONNET: P. Cruttwell
ENGLISH SERMONS: Arthur Pollard
ENGLISH TRANSLATORS AND TRANSLATIONS: J. M. Cohen
ENGLISH TRAVELLERS IN THE NEAR EAST: Robin Fedden
THREE WOMEN DIARISTS: M. Willy

Sixteenth Century and Earlier:

BACON: J. Max Patrick
BEAUMONT & FLETCHER: Ian Fletcher
CHAUCER: Nevill Coghill
GOWER & LYDGATE: Derek Pearsall
HOOKER: Arthur Pollard
KYD: Philip Edwards
LANGLAND: Nevill Coghill
LYLY & PEELE: G. K. Hunter
MALORY: M. C. Bradbrook
MARLOWE: Philip Henderson
MORE: E. E. Reynolds
RALEGH: Agnes Latham
SIDNEY: Kenneth Muir
SKELTON: Peter Green
SPENSER: Rosemary Freeman
TWO SCOTS CHAUCERIANS: H. Harvey Wood
WYATT: Sergio Baldi

Seventeenth Century:

BROWNE: Peter Green
BUNYAN: Henri Talon
CAVALIER POETS: Robin Skelton
CONGREVE: Bonamy Dobrée
DONNE: Frank Kermode
DRYDEN: Bonamy Dobrée
ENGLISH DIARISTS: Evelyn and Pepys: M. Willy
FARQUHAR: A. J. Farmer
JOHN FORD: Clifford Leech
HERBERT: T. S. Eliot
HERRICK: John Press
HOBBES: T. E. Jessop
BEN JONSON: J. B. Bamborough
LOCKE: Maurice Cranston
MARVELL: John Press
MILTON: E. M. W. Tillyard
RESTORATION COURT POETS: V. de S. Pinto
SHAKESPEARE: C. J. Sisson
CHRONICLES: Clifford Leech
EARLY COMEDIES: Derek Traversi
LATER COMEDIES: G. K. Hunter
FINAL PLAYS: Frank Kermode
HISTORIES: L. C. Knights
POEMS: F. T. Prince
PROBLEM PLAYS: Peter Ure
ROMAN PLAYS: T. J. B. Spencer
GREAT TRAGEDIES: Kenneth Muir
THREE METAPHYSICAL POETS: Margaret Willy
WALTON: Margaret Bottrall
WEBSTER: Ian Scott-Kilvert
WYCHERLEY: P. F. Vernon

Eighteenth Century:

BERKELEY: T. E. Jessop
BLAKE: Kathleen Raine
BOSWELL: P. A. W. Collins
BURKE: T. E. Utley
BURNS: David Daiches
WM COLLINS: Oswald Doughty
COWPER: N. Nicholson
CRABBE: R. L. Brett
DEFOE: J. R. Sutherland
FIELDING: John Butt
GAY: Oliver Warner
GIBBON: C. V. Wedgwood
GOLDSMITH: A. Norman Jeffares

GRAY: R. W. Ketton-Cremer
HUME: Montgomery Belgion
SAMUEL JOHNSON: S. C. Roberts
POPE: Ian Jack
RICHARDSON: R. F. Brissenden
SHERIDAN: W. A. Darlington
SMART: Geoffrey Grigson
SMOLLETT: Laurence Brander
STEELE, ADDISON: A. R. Humphreys
STERNE: D. W. Jefferson
SWIFT: J. Middleton Murry (1955)
SWIFT: A. Norman Jeffares (1976)
VANBRUGH: Bernard Harris
HORACE WALPOLE: Hugh Honour

Nineteenth Century:

ARNOLD: Kenneth Allott
AUSTEN: S. Townsend Warner (1951)
AUSTEN: B. C. Southam (1975)
BAGEHOT: N. St John-Stevas
THE BRONTË SISTERS: Phyllis Bentley (1950)
THE BRONTËS: I & II: Winifred Gérin
E. B. BROWNING: Alethea Hayter
ROBERT BROWNING: John Bryson
SAMUEL BUTLER: G. D. H. Cole
BYRON: I, II & III: Bernard Blackstone
CARLYLE: David Gascoyne
CARROLL: Derek Hudson
CLOUGH: Isobel Armstrong
COLERIDGE: Kathleen Raine
CREEVEY & GREVILLE: J. Richardson
DE QUINCEY: Hugh Sykes Davies
DICKENS: K. J. Fielding
EARLY NOVELS: Trevor Blount
LATER NOVELS: Barbara Hardy
DISRAELI: Paul Bloomfield
GEORGE ELIOT: Lettice Cooper
FITZGERALD: Joanna Richardson
GASKELL: Miriam Allott
GISSING: A. C. Ward
HARDY: R. A. Scott-James and C. Day Lewis
HAZLITT: J. B. Priestley
HOOD: Laurence Brander
HOPKINS: Geoffrey Grigson
T. H. HUXLEY: William Irvine
KEATS: Edmund Blunden (1950)
KEATS: Miriam Allott (1976)
LAMB: Edmund Blunden
LANDOR: G. Rostrevor Hamilton
LEAR: Joanna Richardson
MACAULAY: G. R. Potter
MACAULAY: Kenneth Young
MEREDITH: Phyllis Bartlett
MILL: Maurice Cranston
MORRIS: Philip Henderson
NEWMAN: J. M. Cameron
PATER: Ian Fletcher
PEACOCK: J. I. M. Stewart
CHRISTINA ROSSETTI: G. Battiscombe
D. G. ROSSETTI: Oswald Doughty
RUSKIN: Peter Quennell
SCOTT: Ian Jack
SHELLEY: G. M. Matthews
SOUTHEY: Geoffrey Carnall
STEPHEN: Phyllis Grosskurth
STEVENSON: G. B. Stern
SWINBURNE: Ian Fletcher
TENNYSON: B. C. Southam
THACKERAY: Laurence Brander
FRANCIS THOMPSON: Peter Butter
TROLLOPE: Hugh Sykes Davies
WILDE: James Laver
WORDSWORTH: Helen Darbishire

Twentieth Century:

ACHEBE: A. Ravenscroft
ARDEN: Glenda Leeming
AUDEN: Richard Hoggart
BECKETT: J-J. Mayoux
BENNETT: Frank Swinnerton (1950)
BENNETT: Kenneth Young (1975)
BETJEMAN: John Press
BLUNDEN: Alec M. Hardie
BOND: Simon Trussler
BRIDGES: John Sparrow
BURGESS: Carol M. Dix
CAMPBELL: David Wright

CARY: Walter Allen
CHESTERTON: C. Hollis
CHURCHILL: John Connell
COLLINGWOOD: E. W. F. Tomlin
COMPTON-BURNETT: R. Glynn Grylls
CONRAD: Oliver Warner
DE LA MARE: Kenneth Hopkins
NORMAN DOUGLAS: Ian Greenlees
LAWRENCE DURRELL: G. S. Fraser
T. S. ELIOT: M. C. Bradbrook
T. S. ELIOT: The Making of 'The Waste Land': M. C. Bradbrook
FORD MADOX FORD: Kenneth Young
FORSTER: Rex Warner
FRY: Derek Stanford
GALSWORTHY: R. H. Mottram
GOLDING: Stephen Medcalf
GRAVES: M. Seymour-Smith
GRAHAM GREENE: Francis Wyndham
HARTLEY: Paul Bloomfield
A. E. HOUSMAN: Ian Scott-Kilvert
TED HUGHES: Keith Sagar
ALDOUS HUXLEY: Jocelyn Brooke
ISHERWOOD: Francis King
HENRY JAMES: Michael Swan
HANSFORD JOHNSON: Isabel Quigly
JOYCE: J. I. M. Stewart
KIPLING: Bonamy Dobrée
LARKIN: Alan Brownjohn
D. H. LAWRENCE: Kenneth Young
D. H. LAWRENCE I: J. F. C. Littlewood
LESSING: Michael Thorpe
C. DAY LEWIS: Clifford Dyment
WYNDHAM LEWIS: E. W. F. Tomlin
MACDIARMID: Edwin Morgan
MACKENZIE: K. Young
MACNEICE: John Press
MANSFIELD: Ian Gordon
MASEFIELD: L. A. G. Strong
MAUGHAM: J. Brophy
GEORGE MOORE: A. Norman Jeffares
MURDOCH: A. S. Byatt
NAIPAUL: Michael Thorpe
NARAYAN: William Walsh
NEWBY: G. S. Fraser
O'CASEY: W. A. Armstrong
ORWELL: Tom Hopkinson
OSBORNE: Simon Trussler
OWEN: Dominic Hibberd
PINTER: John Russell Taylor
POETS OF THE 1939–45 WAR: R. N. Currey
POWELL: Bernard Bergonzi
POWYS BROTHERS: R. C. Churchill
PRIESTLEY: Ivor Brown
PROSE WRITERS OF WORLD WAR I: M. S. Greicus
HERBERT READ: Francis Berry
SHAFFER: John Russell Taylor
SHAW: A. C. Ward
EDITH SITWELL: John Lehmann
SNOW: William Cooper
SPARK: Patricia Stubbs
STOPPARD: C. W. E. Bigsby
STOREY: John Russell Taylor
SYNGE & LADY GREGORY: E. Coxhead
DYLAN THOMAS: G. S. Fraser
G. M. TREVELYAN: J. H. Plumb
WAR POETS: 1914–18: E. Blunden
EVELYN WAUGH: Christopher Hollis
WELLS: Kenneth Young
WESKER: Glenda Leeming
PATRICK WHITE: R. F. Brissenden
ANGUS WILSON: K. W. Gransden
VIRGINIA WOOLF: B. Blackstone
YEATS: G. S. Fraser